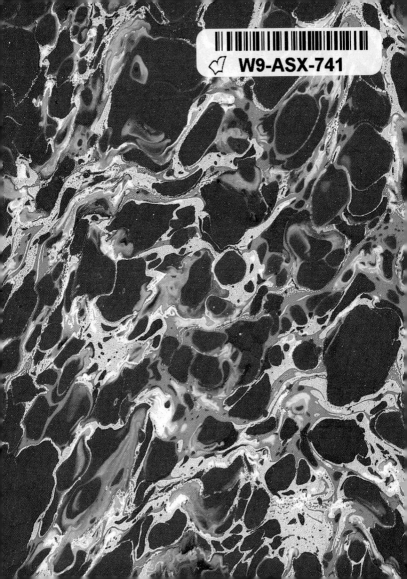

W9-ASX-741

1989

Merry Christmas!

to Marty!

Love from Phyl!

THE BANTAM LIBRARY
of Culinary Arts

TEAS & Tisanes

JILL NORMAN
GWEN EDMONDS

BANTAM BOOKS

TORONTO · NEW YORK · LONDON · SYDNEY · AUCKLAND

TEAS & TISANES

A BANTAM BOOK/PUBLISHED BY ARRANGEMENT WITH
DORLING KINDERSLEY LIMITED

PRINTING HISTORY
DORLING KINDERSLEY EDITION
PUBLISHED IN GREAT BRITAIN IN 1989

BANTAM EDITION/MAY 1989

EDITOR GWEN EDMONDS
DESIGNER JOANNA MARTIN
PHOTOGRAPHER DAVE KING

ART DIRECTOR STUART JACKMAN

LIBRARY OF CONGRESS CATALOGUING-IN-PRODUCTION DATA

NORMAN. JILL.
TEAS & TISANES/JILL NORMAN – BANTAM ED.
P. CM. – (THE BANTAM LIBRARY OF CULINARY ARTS).
INCLUDES INDEX.
1. TEA. 2. HERBAL TEAS. I. TITLE. II. TITLE: TEAS & TISANES. III. SERIES.
TX415.N67 1989 641.3'372–DC19 88-7771
ISBN 0-553-05378-7

PRINTED AND BOUND IN HONG KONG
0 9 8 7 6 5 4 3 2 1

C O N T E N T S

INTRODUCTION

THE TEA BUSH, CAMELLIA SINENSIS, *related to our garden camellia, is the cultivated form of a small evergreen tree with dark glossy leaves which probably originated in the mountain forests along the border of Burma and India with China. In the wild it reaches about 30 feet (10 m) in height but the cultivated plant is constantly pruned to keep it down to at most 5 feet (1.5 m) – this not only makes plucking the leaves easier but also encourages greater leaf production. Cultivation, however, is mostly from seed obtained from trees left to develop naturally.*

Tea pickers can pick up to 60 or 70 lbs a day

Tea is successfully grown from sea level up to some 7000 feet (2200 m) and from the equator to a latitude of about 45° (the Black Sea coast of Russia and parts of northern China and Japan) but always on acid soil with heavy rainfall, and the best results are obtained at altitudes above 4000 feet (1200 m). Plucking is done by hand, despite many attempts to develop the right machinery. Every 7 to 14 days the bud and two terminal leaves are taken off each shoot: an experienced picker can gather up to 60 or even 70 lbs (27-32 kg) a day. In warmer climates (Sri Lanka, for instance) the bush will start yielding in its fourth year and harvesting can go on all year round, but at higher altitudes or in otherwise cooler regions plants may need up to 10 years to mature, and plucking will be limited to a growing season. The producing life of a bush is at least 50 years.

PROCESSING

There are three distinct types of tea: green, oolong, and black. Black teas account for around 98 per cent of all exports to the West. For a long time the importing consumers believed the different types to come from different plants, but it is the method of processing the leaves that produces the characteristics of each tea. Processing is carried out as soon as possible after the harvest and nearly always on the estate. The manufacturing of tea is now highly mechanized, machines carry out the labor intensive tasks of rolling and sieving the leaves.

*Ariel view of tea estate
with taller shade trees*

WITHERING– the newly plucked leaves are spread on trays and fresh or heated air is directed over them for up to 24 hours; the leaves will lose about 40% of their weight.

ROLLING – breaks up the leaf cells, releasing the essential oils and enzymes.

SIEVING – vibrating sieves separate the finer leaves from the coarser elements, which are then rolled and sieved again.

FERMENTING – the full process of oxidization in a humid atmosphere usually takes no more than 4 hours. During this time the color of the tea will change to a rusty brown. Green tea, much used in China and Japan, skips the fermenting stage altogether. Tea fermented only for a very short while is known as oolong.

FIRING – the halting of fermentation by means of very hot air gets the tea ready for storage and transportation.

GRADING

The basic grades of tea are "leaf" and "broken" – the latter giving a darker and more strongly flavored liquor which has become the more popular. The grading is not an indication of quality, only of size and appearance. Broken teas are graded: Broken Orange Pekoe, Broken Pekoe, Broken Pekoe Souchong, Fannings, Dust. Leaf teas are graded as Orange Pekoe, Pekoe, and Souchong. There are also some "Tippy" or "Flowery" grades, applied almost exclusively to Darjeelings. Large leafed teas containing a high proportion of buds; they are picked at the beginning of the season.

Dust: the very finest siftings, now used in tea bags

Orange Pekoe: long thin leaves

Fannings: smallest broken leaf grade producing a rich liquor

Golden Flowery Orange Pekoe: an early picked Darjeeling

Broken Orange Pekoe: contains some of the golden leaf tips

First Flush: Darjeeling grade, the first pluckings of the year

Pekoe: small leaves producing a stronger liquor

Souchong: broad leaves producing a less delicate liquor, often smoked

TRADING

Tea cannot be stored for very long in the tropics without deteriorating, so the journey to the consumer starts after grading.

London and Amsterdam are the traditional auction places for Europe and America, but more tea is auctioned in the producing countries, especially at Colombo and Calcutta. Samples of each kind are made available to the tasters in uniformly brewed pots with both the dry and the infused leaf displayed by their side. The taster reports to the blender, but brokers do the actual buying and selling.

BLENDING

Assam

Yunnan

Darjeeling

Ceylon

*English
Breakfast Blend*

Almost all the black tea in the retail trade is blended, to ensure consistency of taste, quality, and price for any particular brand. Tea varies even within one estate with the weather, and hazards of processing and transportation. In the 18th century, when tea was sold loose, the retailing grocer would make up a blend to the customer's requirements.

PACKAGING

Tisane tea bag

Standard tea bag

Adulteration of tea by coloring, mixing with other vegetable substances, even the reuse of tea leaves eventually caused so many problems that an enterprising merchant made a fortune out of his solution: John Horniman was the first to sell tea in sealed paper packets bearing his name as a guarantee.

Legend has it that the tea bag dates from 1904 when an American tea merchant, Thomas Sullivan, sent out some samples of his wares in little silk bags which his customers found convenient for making tea. Commercially, however, the bag did not catch on until the 1920s and only conquered England in the 1950s.

An unusual form of packaging was developed for the caravan routes to Russia and the even more hazardous transport to Tibet: compressed tablets as hard as stone, much less bulky than loose tea. Shavings from such tablets are boiled in water.

To preserve its flavor loose tea should be kept in an airtight and lightproof container at room temperature, never in glass or plastic or in the refrigerator.

Tea brick

WAYS OF DRINKING TEA

In China and Japan, where tea drinking has the longest history, green tea is the norm and nothing is added.

The West originally also knew only green tea, but as early as 1660 there were recommendations in England for it "being prepared and drank with milk and water," and later it became customary to add sugar as well.

The American colonies proclaimed their independence by rejecting the milk habit, and eventually went one further by inventing iced tea. In Australia the "billy," the can used in the outback for boiling water, has entered national folklore as a tea kettle although it was used just as much for cooking vegetables and stews. Morocco is the only country outside the Far East where green tea is widely drunk, with a liberal dose of sugar and fresh spearmint leaves added. The Russians use a samovar, a water heater on top of which a small teapot is kept with a very strong tea essence. A little of

Russian tea drinkers with samovar

this essence is dispensed in small tea glasses and topped up with water from the samovar. In Turkey a similar essence is used.

In Tibet, where tea consumption is very high, chips from a tea brick are put in cold water which is then boiled for hours. Before serving salt is added and a piece of rancid yak butter. The tea is served in small wooden bowls.

*C*HINA IS THE ORIGINAL *home of tea; it has been cultivated there for more than 1500 years. China dominated the tea trade until the 1850s, after which its decline was dramatic. However, it still produces the most wonderful variety of teas; black, green, and oolong are all manufactured commercially along with smoked and scented teas. Tea is now produced on a cooperative system, processed at local factories, and tea for export is subject to strict quality control, which means a standardization from year to year.*

Generally the black teas are delicate and best drunk without milk, but perhaps with lemon.

Yunnan: prized for its health-giving properties, one of the strongest China blacks

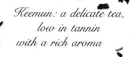

Keemun: a delicate tea, low in tannin with a rich aroma

Bamboo: a strong, bitter tea packed in dried bamboo leaves

Ichang: a small leaf tea producing a tea with a slightly smoky taste

Russian Caravan: a blend based on fine China blacks, traditional to the Russian caravan traders

Chingwoo: tightly rolled tea producing a red liquor and fine aroma

CHINA – *Smoked, Green, and Oolong*

THE FIRST TEA to reach the West was green tea, and only in the 19th century did the stronger blacks displace it in popular taste. In China such a change never took place.

Lapsang Souchong: one of China's most famous black teas, with a distinctive smoky taste produced by slow firing over wood

Chunmee: a delicate green tea, the everyday tea of the domestic market

Gunpowder: the best quality green tea; small leaves, tightly rolled

China oolongs are produced in Fukien province

Oolongs: semifermented large-leafed teas falling between black and green teas; the best come from Formosa, now, Taiwan.

Formosa oolong Peach Blossom: Oolongs have a delicate fruity taste and are sometimes scented with jasmine, gardenia or rose petals

Formosa oolong Black Dragon

INDIA

*I*NDIA IS THE WORLD'S *largest producer and exporter of tea. The British first planted tea commercially in India in the 1830s. The first plantations were in Assam, an inhospitable district in the northeast of India. Tea is now grown in many areas, much of it of good quality and used extensively in blends. However, there are three areas producing tea of the highest quality: Assam, Darjeeling, and Nilgiri.*

Special Flowery Orange Pekoe: a fine quality Assam

Best Golden Orange Pekoe

A middle grade Assam

Assam, the first and largest area given over to tea planting, produces strong, mature, black teas. The best quality Assams have golden tippy leaves; the medium grades have hard, flinty leaves and form the mainstay of British blending, producing teas with a rich color and flavor, ideal for drinking with milk.

Darjeeling, in the foothills of the Himalayas, produces India's most prized teas. Grown at altitudes of up to 6,500 feet, the bushes may take 10 years to mature. It is possible to buy Darjeeling from individual tea gardens, and the most famous command high prices. Darjeelings have a distinctive "muscatel" flavor.

Tippy Golden Flowery Orange Pekoe: fine quality with tips

Flowery Orange Pekoe: a good quality Darjeeling

1st Flush: the most expensive and sought after Darjeeling

Nilgiri is a high plateau in the south of India. Its teas are brisk, with a taste somewhere between the mature Assams in the North and the sharper teas of Ceylon. These teas are used extensively in blending but are of a fine enough quality to be drunk unblended.

Nilgiri

CEYLON

*C*EYLON (SRI LANKA) *is the world's third largest producer and second largest exporter of tea. Tea was first planted in Ceylon in 1867 and became the principal cash crop shortly after, when a blight decimated the coffee plantations. Ceylon's teas are synonymous with quality. This is in part due to the genuine high standard of the tea and in part to an unprecedented marketing campaign by early planters and merchants.*

The best quality Ceylon teas are "high grown," on slopes above 4000 feet (1200 m), and many famous unblended teas from individual tea gardens are still available. Ceylon teas are strong but delicate, with a slight bitterness. They are good with milk but not so suited to lemon.

Uva Highland

An early Ceylon tea advertisement

St James Flowery Orange Pekoe

Roehampton

St James Fannings

Ceylon Orange Pekoe

RUSSIA & KENYA

Russia and Kenya began their tea plantations early this century. Russia's teas are full-bodied and fragrant; Kenya's are reddish with a brisk taste.

Russian

Kenyan

JAPAN

*"Tea with us became more than an idealization
of the form of drinking; it is a religion of the art
of life." Okakura's The Book of Tea*

*"Devotees of Cha-no-yu appreciate Art and
worship Nature through the medium of the
indescribably delicate and refreshing aroma of
powdered tea."
Fukukita, The Tea Cult of Japan*

TEA HAS BEEN GROWN *and drunk in Japan since the 8th or 9th century. The country produces almost exclusively green teas, for which the domestic demand is so great that little is exported.*

Tea has long played an important part in Japanese social life. From an early date its popularity was closely associated with the rise of Zen Buddhism, the monks adopting tea drinking as part of their ceremonial life.

The tea ceremony as it is practiced these days was outlined by the teacher Rikyu in the mid-16th century. The ceremony normally involves a host and four guests, and takes place in

*Utamaro, Courtesan
Okita
of Naniwa-ya Teahouse*

a specially built tea house in a secluded part of the garden. First a light meal is served, and after a break the main part of the ceremony: the drinking of a thick liquor made from powdered green tea. Finally a thin tea is served. Correct procedure is rigorously observed.

The purpose of the ceremony, as with much Zen thinking, is simple: to calm the mind through concentration.

Bancha: the everyday tea, low in caffeine

Tencha: the very best, used for the tea ceremony

Genmaicha: panfried rolled green leaf with toasted rice

Sencha: a better quality tea of which some is exported

EXOTIC TEAS

*T*HE CHINESE HAVE *produced scented teas for cen-turies using their abundant flowers, fruits, and oils. They are best drunk without milk but can be sweetened with honey or sugar. The spiced teas make warming winter drinks, flower teas are light and refreshing, and the fruit teas make excellent iced tea.*

Earl Grey is the most famous scented tea in the West. The original recipe was given to the second Earl Grey in 1830 by a Chinese mandarin. It is a blend of fine black teas flavored with the oil of the bergamot orange.

Earl Grey

Rum

Almond

Green Mint

Spice

Ginger

Caramel

Vanilla and lavender

Honey

FRUIT TEAS

Apple

Lemon

Mango

Coconut

FLOWER TEAS

Rose   Jasmine

Orange blossom   Lotus flower

TISANES

*T*ISANES OR HERB TEAS *have been drunk for centuries, sometimes as medicine, sometimes for refreshment. They can be made from almost any edible plant, and you may need as much as 2 table-spoons of a fresh herb or 1 tablespoon of dried, per cup.*

Tisanes from flowers or leaves can be made in the same way as an ordinary pot of tea, but those made from tougher material need to be boiled for up to 5 minutes, then steeped for a further 10-20 minutes to allow the flavor to develop.

Rose petal and hibiscus flower: a pretty, sharp-tasting infusion

Elderflower: a mild stimulant

German chamomile: one of the most popular tisanes, a carminative, ideal for a nightcap

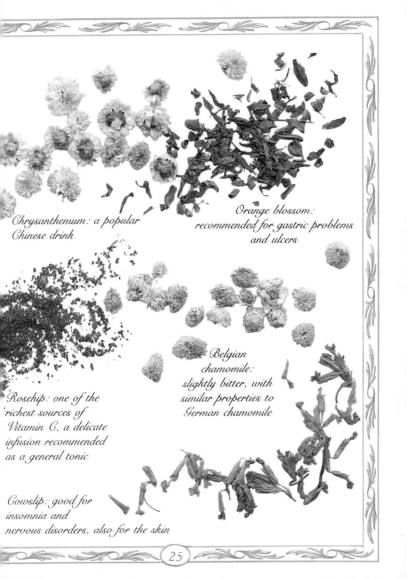

Chrysanthemum: a popular Chinese drink

Orange blossom: recommended for gastric problems and ulcers

Belgian chamomile: slightly bitter, with similar properties to German chamomile

Rosehip: one of the richest sources of Vitamin C, a delicate infusion recommended as a general tonic

Cowslip: good for insomnia and nervous disorders, also for the skin

TISANES

Nettle: harvest leaves before June;
relieves rheumatic pain

Thyme and cinnamon: good for
the easing of colds and coughs

Fennel: good as a
blood cleanser; boil
the seeds for 5 minutes

Lime blossom:
used to
ease headaches

Peppermint: refreshing;
good for headaches and
as a stomach settler

TISANES

Rosemary: good if you are feeling low

Mixed fruit: a refreshing drink warm or iced

Maté: drunk in South America, it contains caffeine

Lemon Verbena: reduces fever, eases rheumatic pain

Raspberry Leaf: an ancient remedy for easing childbirth

The history of tea

CHINA IS THE *home of tea;* it is known that tea was cultivated there nearly 2000 years ago. By AD 800 when Lu Yu wrote his Book of Tea (Ch'a Ching) its use had spread to Japan, and not much later small quantities were taken west on the Persian caravan routes. The Venetians knew about tea by the middle of the 16th century, but only as a medicine for stomach troubles and gout, leaving it to their budding trade rivals, the Dutch, to introduce tea into Europe.

This they did in 1606 when the first shipment of China tea reached Amsterdam. Although an expensive novelty at first, it soon became the most popular beverage in the country. Success in the export market was varied. In France the craze was early but short-lived; England's acceptance was slow but lasting. In 1658 the first advertisement for tea appeared in an English paper; in 1660 Samuel Pepys "did send for a cup of tee, a China drink, of which I never had drunk before." In 1664 the East India Company made Charles II a present of tea, in 1689 it began to import tea direct from China, and in 1721 it was given a monopoly on the tea trade that was to last until 1833.

In 1834 the East India Company's China monopoly ended – in fact, the whole Company was wound up. The immediate cause of this lay in rapid expansion of the new Indian Empire; public opinion saw it as a way of getting better tea at more reasonable prices.

Assam was the first region to begin tea cultivation in a promising way, using a wild native strain discovered in 1823, a year after the Society of Arts had offered a gold medal for successful propagation in any Indian colony. Production became really successful by 1852 and other north Indian districts (Darjeeling, Cachar) soon followed. Attempts were made in other places, too, but the first truly spectacular entrant after Assam was Ceylon, which completely replaced its blighted coffee plantations with tea in the 1870s. Around the same time the Dutch colonists started plantations in Java, which would become the third largest producers of export tea. In 1849 the laws barring American ships from competing on the China to England run had been repealed, and the fast New England clipper ships out-sailed the older Aberdeen-built boats by as much as four days.

The first tea of the season had always commanded a premium, but the Tea Races of the 1860s added the excitement of extensive betting among the public. The opening of the Suez canal in 1869 and the growing use of steam power ended this romantic era. Meanwhile the British public had reacted favorably to the much stronger teas of India and by 1900 imports from China were only 5% of the total — due in part to Chinese reluctance to improve quality, transport, and price. Ceylon teas became fashionable in the 1890s after

TEA AND THE ENGLISH

When tea was first introduced into England, it was in the newly established coffee houses, which were male preserves. Once the novelty wore off, although the price remained high, tea found its way into the home.

The decline of the coffee houses saw the rise of the tea garden both in England and America. Until the mid 19th century these parks on the outskirts of the city offered family entertainment (concerts, illuminations, games, and fireworks) and provided tea as the drink suitable for all the family.

On the domestic front meanwhile a quiet revolution had taken place. Dinner, the main meal of the day, originally taken at noon, had gradually been getting later, until in the 18th century it would be at 3 or 4 in the

some unprecedentedly aggressive marketing of unblended teas and specially selected grades such as Golden Tips. Other producing regions have since entered the market, notably in Africa (Malawi, Kenya, Uganda, Tanganyika) and South America (Argentina, itself now a tea-drinking country).

afternoon. In the early evening came the tea hour, the polite visiting time. By the early 19th century the two had changed place, with "tea and cream and butter'd rolls" filling the space between breakfast and the evening meal.

The tea shop or tea room was born in the 1880s, when the Aerated Bread Company and most enduringly Lyons recognized and exploited an obvious gap for light refreshments.

TEA WARE

The earliest known tea pots were, of course, Chinese. The small unglazed red stoneware pots made at Yi-Hsing near Shanghai from around 1500 have the characteristic shape, with lid and spout, imitated throughout the western world. In fact the shape had nothing to do with the tea-making (the Chinese boiled their tea in an iron kettle) but was copied from earlier wine jars. Yi-Hsing teapots were brought over with the first tea shipments to Holland, and the Delft ceramic industry lost little time trying to copy them but came no further than an inferior earthenware imitation. In England the oldest surviving teapots are made of silver, but the potters also tried their hand. The Elers brothers, who probably came to England in the wake of William III in 1688, were among the first to move to Staffordshire for its clay. Celia Fiennes records seeing "the making of fine teapotts, cups and saucers of the fine red earth" there in 1698.

Lead-glaze, salt-glaze, and enameling produced some fanciful and highly decorative pots, but the fine stoneware of Josiah Wedgwood, stained in a variety of colors and decorated with white cameo reliefs in the new neoclassical mode, revolutionized the industry after 1760 and led to the first real mass production. Wedgwood took the unusual trouble of having all his basic designs tested by his wife, which may well account for their enduring quality. Meanwhile France and Germany tried to solve the riddle of China's other great export: porcelain. Böttger of Dresden took the lead in 1713, and his Meissen factory produced countless complete tea sets more in the style of the south German silversmiths than of any Chinese model. The Sèvres factory in France and the Chelsea workshops both used a softer paste with elaborate painted decorations. In 1800 Josiah Spode first produced what quickly became and still is standard English

porcelain: bone china, an economical hybrid porcelain containing bone ash. It made Spode rich and secured a new lease of life for the Staffordshire potteries.

The 20th century has seen the introduction of new materials such as stainless steel, and a gradual return to the most basic and functional forms – which turn out to be very close to those of the original Yi-Hsing pots.

Recipes

*All recipes are for 4,
but some will serve more*

LEMON TEA

*1¾ pints/1 liter water
2 lemons
2 tablespoons tea*

Boil the water, add the juice of 1 lemon, and pour it over the tea in a pot. Infuse for 3–4 minutes, then fill up the pot with more boiling water. Leave another 3 minutes. Serve in glasses with slices of lemon.

CINNAMON TEA WITH HONEY

*1¾ pints/1 liter water
1 stick cinnamon
2 tablespoons tea
3–4 oz/75–125 g honey*

Boil the water in a pan with the cinnamon stick broken into 2 or 3 pieces. Add the tea leaves, remove from the heat, cover, and infuse for 5 minutes. Strain the tea and stir in honey to taste.

TEA WITH EGGS

"The Jesuite that came from China, Ann. 1664, told Mr. Waller, that there they use sometimes in this manner. To near a pint of the infusion, take *two yolks* of *new laid-eggs*, and beat them very well with as much *fine sugar* as is sufficient for this quantity of liquor; when they are very well incorporated, pour your *tea* upon the eggs and sugar, and stir them well together. So drink it hot. . . . In these parts, he saith, we let the hot water remain too long soaking upon the tea, which makes it extract into itself the earthy parts of the herb. The water is to remain upon it, no longer that whiles you can say the *Miserere* Psalm very leisurely. Then pour it upon the sugar, or sugar and eggs. Thus you have only the spiritual parts of the tea, which is much more active, penetrative and friendly to nature. You may from this regard take a little more of the herb; about one dragm of tea, will serve for a pint of water."

The Closet of Sir Kenelm Digby Knight Opened, 1669

MOROCCAN MINT TEA

1¾ pints/1 liter water
2 tablespoons green tea
a handful of fresh spearmint
4 oz/125 g sugar cubes

Boil the water. Put the tea into a pot and pour on a little water. Swill it around and pour off to remove the dust and some of the tea's bitterness. Add mint and sugar, pour over the remaining hot water, and infuse for 6–7 minutes. Make sure the mint leaves stay below the surface. Serve the tea in small glasses.

Stuffed Prunes

1 lb/500 g large prunes
boiling black tea
2 oz/50 g ground almonds
2 oz/50 g sugar
1 egg yolk
brandy

Pour the boiling tea over the prunes and soak overnight, then simmer the prunes in the tea for about 15 minutes, or until the pits can be removed. Leave the prunes to dry while preparing the marzipan. Mix together the almonds, sugar, and egg yolk, add a dash of brandy and blend until you have a smooth paste. Stuff the prunes with the marzipan and, if you wish, roll them in sugar before serving.

Chinese Tea Eggs

12 eggs
1½ tablespoons black tea leaves
1 pint/600 ml water
1 tablespoon soy sauce
1½ teaspoons salt
1 star anise

Pierce each egg at the blunt end with a pin to prevent the shell cracking when boiled. Put them into a pan, cover with water, bring to the boil, and cook for 10–12 minutes. Lift the eggs out and put them under cold running water for a few minutes. When cold crack the egg shells gently, by tapping them or rolling them on a table: the shells should be cracked all over but should not come loose. Put the eggs back in the pan with all the other ingredients. If there is not enough water to cover them, add a little more. Bring slowly to the boil, then cover and simmer for an hour. Let the eggs cool in the liquid— you may keep them in it for 24 hours to intensify the flavor. Just before serving remove the shells: the eggs will have an attractive appearance of aged porcelain.

SPICED PRUNES

1 lb/500 g prunes
cold black tea
a piece of cinnamon
a blade of mace
6 cloves
6 allspice berries
1 pint/600 ml wine vinegar
8 oz/250 g sugar

Soak the prunes in the tea overnight, then simmer them in the tea until quite soft, about 10–15 minutes. Drain, and reserve the tea. Crush the spices, tie them in a piece of muslin, and boil together with the vinegar and sugar for 5 minutes. Put the prunes into warmed preserving jars. Add ½ pint/300 ml of the tea to the vinegar and bring to the boil again. Remove the bag of spices and pour the liquid over the prunes.

Cover the jars and keep for a week before using. The prunes go well with cold meats, particularly ham and pork.

IRISH TEABRACK

8 oz/250 g raisins
8 oz/250 g golden raisins
8 oz/250 g brown sugar
¼ pint/150 ml strong black tea
8 oz/250 g flour
1 teaspoon baking powder
1 teaspoon pumpkin pie spices
3 eggs

Put the fruit and sugar in a bowl and pour over the tea. Cover and leave to soak overnight. Sift together the flour, baking powder, and spices. Beat the eggs. Add the flour and eggs alternately to the fruit and mix thoroughly. Grease a medium loaf pan, pour in the mixture, and bake in a preheated oven, 160°C, 325°F, for 1½ hours.

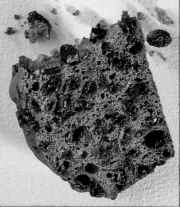

KASHMIRI TEA

1³/4 pints/1 liter water
1 teaspoon green tea
pinch bicarbonate of soda
pinch salt
1/2 pint/300 ml milk

Boil the water, add the tea leaves and bicarbonate of soda. Boil for 5 minutes, then add the salt and the milk. Bring to the boil again, then serve.

CARDAMOM TEA

1³/4 pints/1 liter water
1/4 pint/150 ml milk
2 tablespoons black tea leaves
6 cardamoms crushed

Boil the water and milk separately. Pour both over the tea leaves and cardamoms in a pot. Infuse for 5 minutes.

CAMOMILE NIGHTCAP

Pour *150 ml/1/4 pint boiling water* over *1 teaspoon dried camomile flowers* and *a piece of orange peel* and infuse for 10 minutes in a warm place. Strain and sweeten with a little *honey* if you wish.

SPICED TEA

1³/4 pints/1 liter water
1 stick cinnamon
3 cloves
3 allspice berries
3 cardamoms, crushed
1 tablespoon black tea leaves

Simmer the water and spices for 5 minutes, then bring to the boil and pour onto the tea in a pot. Infuse for 5 minutes.

ICED TEA PUNCH

1/2 pint/300 ml strong black tea
6 oz/175 g sugar
1/2 pint/300 ml orange juice
juice of 2 lemons
1/2 pint/300 ml ginger ale
1 orange, sliced
1 lemon, sliced

Strain the hot tea onto the sugar and let it dissolve. Cool and chill. Mix with the other ingredients just before serving over ice cubes.

GINGER TEA

1 in/2.5 cm piece of ginger
1 pint/600 ml water

Chop the ginger finely. Boil the water and pour it over the ginger. Infuse for 5 minutes.

TEA ICE CREAM

Jasmine and Earl Grey are the teas I like best for making ice cream, but any highly scented tea, including fruit or flower teas, will give a rich and unusual tasting ice cream.

1/2 pint/300 ml light cream or milk
2 tablespoons tea
1 tablespoon rose water (optional)
1/4 pint/150 ml heavy cream
3 egg yolks
3 oz/75 g sugar

Heat the light cream or milk to boiling point, remove from the heat, stir in the tea, cover, and infuse for 5 minutes. Stir in the rose water.

Beat together egg yolks and sugar until pale and thick, then slowly pour in the strained cream, stirring constantly. Heat the mixture in a double boiler (or put the bowl over a pan of simmering water) and stir constantly until it thickens enough to coat the back of a spoon. Do not let it boil or it will curdle.

Cool, then stir in the double cream and freeze in an ice cream machine according to the manufacturer's instructions.

JASMINE TEA AND PEAR SORBET

3/4 pint/450 ml water
2 tablespoons jasmine tea
1 lb/500 g well-flavored ripe pears
4 tablespoons lemon juice
3 oz/75 g sugar

Pour the boiling water over the tea leaves and let it infuse for 20 minutes, then strain. It should be strong.

Peel, core, and chop the pears and put them into a small pan with the lemon juice. Turn them around in the juice so they will not discolor. Add the sugar and the tea and bring to the boil. Stir until the sugar dissolves, then simmer for 10 minutes. Pour the mixture into a blender and puree. Taste, and add more lemon juice and/or sugar if necessary. Cool. Pour into an ice cream machine and freeze according to the manufacturer's instructions.

INDEX

ACKNOWLEDGEMENTS

*Bantam Books
would like to thank the
following people:*

· ILLUSTRATORS ·
JANE THOMSON
SHEILAGH NOBLE

JACKET
· PHOTOGRAPHY ·
JULIE FISHER

FALKINER FINE
PAPERS LTD

THE TEA COUNCIL

· TYPESETTING ·
WYVERN
TYPESETTING LTD

· REPRODUCTION ·
COLOURSCAN
SINGAPORE

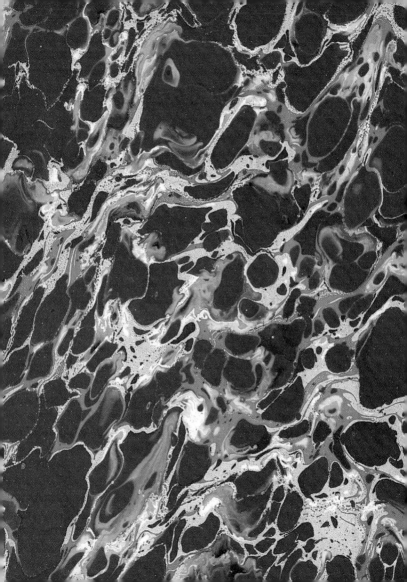